Old Loch Lomondside
by P.J.G. Ransom

By the late 1920s, mass-produced motor cars were enabling many people to achieve a new mobility, but traffic was not yet so heavy as to prevent them from enjoying the open road, and halting where they pleased. This is the main road up the west side of Loch Lomond, a little north of Luss to judge from the appearance of Ben Lomond in the background. The car in the foreground is a two-seater Morris of 1927/28; its dicky seat at the rear is open and, considering the interest being taken by the driver and front-seat passenger, the photographer has just disembarked from it. The two cars parked side-by-side on the loch shore in the middle distance are an Austin of 1927/28 (on the left) and a Morris of 1926/27. The car on the extreme right is a Hudson, made in America.

Text © P.J.G. Ransom, 2007.
First published in the United Kingdom, 2007,
by Stenlake Publishing Ltd.
www.stenlake.co.uk
ISBN 9781840333800

A train for Glasgow Central Low Level enters Balloch Central; the period is the 1950s, or at least sometime after nationalization in 1948 (the locomotive is numbered in a post-nationalisation British Railways series) and before the line was electrified in 1960. The 2-6-2 tank locomotive is of a type built by the London, Midland & Scottish Railway in the late thirties to haul local passenger trains, and the coaches also appear to be of LMS origin. They were intended to carry a lot of passengers over short journeys - each was laid out as a series of full-width compartments with external doors and no corridor. The station appears clean, neat and tidy (untypical of the period!), with hanging flower baskets suspended from the platform awning. The train destination indicator over the platform was changed manually by station staff when necessary. According to the British Transport Commission's handbook of stations (1956), Balloch Central was equipped to handle not only passengers, but also goods, coal, parcels, livestock, horses, prize cattle, and furniture vans, carriages, motor cars, portable engines and 'machines on wheels'. Its goods yard crane was a substantial one, able to lift loads of up to 7 tons. How much use was being made of all of these facilities by that time is another question; motor vehicles had long been well developed and able to go anywhere there was a road.

INTRODUCTION

The most conspicuous changes to Loch Lomondside over the past 100 years have been those brought about by the arrival of the internal combustion engine. The photographs in this book mostly date from the last decade of the nineteenth century and the first few decades of the twentieth. In many cases the buildings and the scenery remain recognisable, but where today there are double yellow lines, these photographs show that at one time the only vehicle to be seen was a horse and cart. Where today there is tarmac with a constant rush of traffic in both directions, there was once a gravelled road so empty that cyclists could ride in a carefree manner along the wrong side. In these near-idyllic scenes there are only a few early motor vehicles. Fast-moving by the standards of the time, they were slow by those of today, although something of the uncrowded, unhurried atmosphere of those days can still be experienced on sections of the former main road up the west side of the loch which have been bypassed but remain in use for local traffic – notably the southern approach to Luss.

By the end of the nineteenth century Loch Lomondside had long been popular with tourists and visitors. They had first arrived a century before and the combination of fine scenery and proximity to the cities and industrial towns of the Lowlands ensured its popularity. In the mid-eighteenth century the narrow horse road up the west shore of the loch had been replaced by the military road, making the district accessible for carriages and carts, and subsequently this itself was further much improved. Inns, which travellers at first found primitive, were transformed into substantial hotels. Loch Lomond itself, which had been used as a waterway for centuries, was well served by steamers. At Balloch trains from Glasgow and Stirling ran onto the pier and steamers berthed alongside. Where neither trains nor steamers could penetrate, horsedrawn coach services survived.

The harbinger of approaching change was the arrival of the bicycle in the 1890s. Cycling rapidly became popular, both for short distances and for long tours. Primitive motor cars, motor cycles and motor buses appeared in the early 1900s; buses and motor lorries based on redundant military vehicles appeared in quantity after the First World War and mass-produced cars soon after that. Pneumatic tyres sucked the dust out of road surfaces so that water could penetrate; succeeding vehicles deepened puddles into potholes. The solution was to bind road surfaces with tar.

Some changes came and went quickly. The electric tram was introduced to Balloch in 1908, but had been eclipsed by the motor bus only twenty years later. One of Balloch's two railways lost its passenger trains in the 1930s, and the winter steamer service on the loch was also withdrawn that decade. But more evident was a long period of coexistence between old forms of transport and new. Horsedrawn coaches were still a feature of Inversnaid in the late 1930s. On the main railway approach to Balloch steam trains were still running in the 1950s, and paddle steamers still sailed the loch, even though motor cars, motor buses and motor boats were by then commonplace.

The banks and islands of Loch Lomond have been inhabited since prehistoric times. The islands in particular offered security from wild animals and hostile tribes; during the Iron Age and later, many inhabitants lived on crannogs, artificial islands which offered the same advantages. At a much later period still, the contrast between the lowlands around the southern end of the loch and the highlands of its northern part was much more than topographical; there was a strong cultural divide too - different society, different style of housing, different language. However, by the early 1900s only echoes of those differences remained. In comparatively recent years, perhaps the most notable change has been the decline in the importance of the 'big house' and the growth, in quantity and quality, of many smaller ones. That is a reflection of narrowing distinctions of social class and wealth. Buildings are often surprisingly little changed, even though their function may have altered. With a few exceptions there seems to have been little demolition and reconstruction although hotels have in many cases been extended. To revisit the locations of these photographs is often to find the man-made surroundings familiar. The same applies even more to the natural surroundings, to the outline of the hills and the ever-changing patterns of light and shade upon them, and to the regular progress of the seasons. The illustrations which follow are laid out according to successive seasons – although, as befits a tourist area, most by far are of summer scenes.

ACKNOWLEDGEMENTS

I am most grateful to those who have helped in one way or another with information. In particular, Bob Flockhart, of the Museum of Transport, Glasgow, has identified many of the vintage vehicles which appear in the photographs, and told me the story of James Robertson and his car engine; Graham Hopner, Information Services Librarian at Dumbarton Library, once again drew on his encyclopaedic knowledge of the district, with particular reference to Tullichewan Castle; Janet Beveridge of Kilmaronock Heritage Group and her associates have delved into long memories to provide most useful information; Nicola McCrae of the Scottish Youth Hostels Association provided the stories of Loch Lomond and Inverbeg hostels; and Donna Siems of Loch Lomond Golf Club told me about Rossdhu past and present. My wife Elisabeth and agent Duncan McAra have been as supportive as ever.

During the hard winters of the nineteenth century Loch Lomond was frozen on several occasions: in 1814, 1838, 1855, 1879, 1881 and 1895. In 1838 the ice was bearing for a fortnight at the end of February, and in 1895 – when this photograph was taken - for even longer, from the end of January until 23 February. On 15 February a bonspiel attracted over 200 curlers from eighteen clubs.

In 1895 the frozen loch attracted huge quantities of skaters and sightseers and the paddle steamer *Prince of Wales*, frozen in at Balloch Pier, was opened up as a stationary restaurant. Yet so spacious is the loch that a Glasgow journalist, skating from Luss to Balloch in the early morning, passed only one other skater en route.

Left: Some of the best views around the loch can be seen early in the year, before they become concealed by lochside vegetation. In this photograph, taken in January 1929, the peak of Ben Lomond is framed by trees.

Above: The falls of Inversnaid, which descend into the loch itself, had been made famous by William Wordsworth in his poem 'To the Highland Girl …' and became a magnet for Victorian tourists. There has long been a footbridge over this spot; today it carries the West Highland Way.

Springtime tasks on the banks of the loch: on the left seed is being cast by hand, while on the right horsedrawn harrows are being used to break up the ground, either preparatory to sowing, or to cover over the seed once sown.

SOWING AND HARROWING, LOCH LOMOND.
H.R.8.

Loch Lomond paddle steamers operated throughout the year in Edwardian times for the benefit of local travellers, parcels and mails, rather than tourists. In this photograph one of the steamers is getting away from Tarbet Pier, built in the late 1840s, on what looks to have been a cold, clear day in early spring.

When Dorothy and William Wordsworth came to Tarbet in 1803 the inn was simple and the staff were Gaelic speaking. By the end of the nineteenth century it had been replaced by the substantial Victorian hotel seen here. In summer it bustles with visitors, but in this springtime photograph there is little sign of activity. The hotel's horse omnibus is parked under the tree: the steamer pier is nearby so probably the bus was used to take guests to and from Arrochar & Tarbet Station, and Arrochar Pier on Loch Long. Today, the foreground of this picture is part of a busy junction of trunk roads.

As can be seen here, little has changed in the natural surroundings of Loch Lomond. This was Tarbet, photographed on a sunny evening in 1913 as the shadows of swiftly moving clouds dappled the hillsides. The roofs of the hotel emerge from the trees in the middle distance, and Loch Lomond can be seen over to the right. The course of the West Highland Railway is clear, along the slopes on the left. The line had been completed a couple of decades earlier.

To judge from the quantity of boats present in this early season view, Balmaha was already a popular mooring place by the 1930s, although nothing like so popular as it has since become. The steam yacht *Violet* of earlier times – see page 14 – has since disappeared and a handsome motor cruiser, typical of the period, is lying at a mooring in the middle of the bay. Through the topmost branches of the tree in the centre the Balmaha Tearoom can be seen. It was built around 1930 and was burned beyond by repair by a fire in 1971.

The south-west corner of Inchmurrin island, largest in Loch Lomond and inhabited over many centuries. The castle – the ruins of which can be seen clearly between the trees in the centre – was built in the late fourteenth century by the Earls of Lennox as a retreat from pestilence and Highland clansmen, both then being unwelcome visitors to their mainland territories. In the fifteenth century it was home to the tragic figure of the Isabella, Duchess of Albany. Her husband, the Duke of Albany and Regent of Scotland, together with their two sons and her father the Earl of Lennox, had all been beheaded on the same day on the orders of King James I. James had been brought up a virtual prisoner at the English court and on his eventual return north considered that the Regent and his family had betrayed him in his absence. Isabella, however, was allowed to live out her widowhood on the island. The island eventually passed into the ownership of the Dukes of Montrose.

The island of Inchmurrin was for many years used by the Dukes of Montrose as a deer park, a herd of fallow deer being kept there for stalking. There was a resident keeper, for whom this neat lodge was built early in the nineteenth century. By the 1890s the *New Oarsman's Guide*, published by the Cruising Club, was advising readers that Inchmurrin was the first place, as they headed up the loch, at which they might land and camp. They were advised to ask permission from the keeper, 'who can usually supply milk and any little necessaries which the camper may have forgotten.'

The view from Balmaha. The Duke of Montrose's steam yacht *Violet* is lying on her accustomed mooring where she was a familiar sight from the 1880s until the First World War. To the right is the point leading to Balmaha steamer pier round the corner; in the background is the island of Inchcailloch with its oakwoods.

Paddle steamer *Prince Edward* - which served lochside residents and visitors from 1912 until 1954 when she was withdrawn and broken up - calling at Balmaha Pier on her way up the loch. Conic Hill is in the background.

There were burials on Inchcailloch from the earliest times until the 1940s. The island has a long history of religious associations: St Kentigerna founded a nunnery here in the eighth century, and later Inchcailloch Parish Church was on the island for five centuries or so; a mainland church was eventually provided in the seventeenth century and the parish was renamed Buchanan, but the burial ground continued in use. MacGregor and MacFarlane are prominent among the names of those buried here.

A bullnose Morris and other vintage vehicles and bicycles awaiting the arrival of the steamer at Balmaha Pier. Built in the late 1840s, the pier is half a mile or so from the village proper, which evidently made some form of transport desirable.

Houseboats became popular on Loch Lomond in the 1920s. The main concentration was at Balloch, but Aldochlay Bay, south of Luss and seen here, was another popular location. At least three of the houseboats in view appear to be conversions of ship's lifeboats. Swan Island – partly hidden by the nearest boat but supporting full-size trees – is a crannog, a small artificial island which once offered security to Iron Age inhabitants.

Waiting for the steamer at Luss in the late 1920s – the pier building is on the right, although the pier itself is out of the picture. Ben Lomond forms the backdrop. The car on the left is a three-seater 'clover-leaf' Citroën – there were two seats in the front and one at the back on the centre-line of the car.

André Citroën, along with Herbert Austin and William Morris, understood the benefits of mass production as practised by Henry Ford. It looks as though his dealers were successful in popularising his light, cheap cars in the Loch Lomond area, for here is another 'clover-leaf' three-seater parked in the main street of Luss, fifty yards or so from the one shown in the previous picture. Then, as now, the village gardens were famously bright with roses and tropaeolum.

Travelling north up Loch Lomondside in 1803, Dorothy Wordsworth and her brother William came to Luss, the first Highland settlement they encountered and one where, she wrote in her journal, 'we first saw houses without windows, the smoke coming out of the open window-places; the chimneys were like stools with four legs, a hole being left in the (thatched) roof for the smoke, and over that a slate placed upon four sticks'. Those simple long houses were demolished in the mid-nineteenth century. The landowner, Colquhoun of Luss, replaced them with the attractive single-story dwellings seen in these pictures and they remain familiar – indeed famous – today. In this picture dating from the early 1920s a solid-tyre motor charabanc, thought to be of Star manufacture, makes its way between them. Pedestrians disappearing down the road are probably heading for the steamer pier.

Then, as now, a short straight street linked Luss Hotel in the background with the main village behind the photographer. The approaching van is a Daimler, probably a bus chassis with a van body. Such vehicles were often used by food manufacturers for wholesale deliveries to grocers, which may well be the task upon which it is here engaged.

Despite the evident popularity of motor vehicles around Luss in the 1920s, there was still horsedrawn traffic to be seen. The leader of this pony with its cartie appears to have a badge suspended from his left lapel, and so is possibly carrying out some officially recognised task – probably delivering parcels which have arrived on the steamer, or carrying the mails between steamer and post office.

Luss Hotel in the late 1920s. Behind the open touring car is a Ford motor bus, which is likely to be a service bus operated by Elliott's of Balloch. Motor bus services reached Loch Lomondside villages in the 1920s and as a consequence the winter steamer service on the loch was discontinued from 1933. By the late 1930s the hotel had become the Colquhoun Arms, the name it still carries. In 1937 the AA awarded it one star. Single rooms were between 6s. and 7s. 6d. a night, including a bath but excluding breakfast which was another 3s. The bar, according to licensing hours then in force, closed at 9.30 p.m. in summer and 9 p.m. in winter.

Balloch Station now occupies the foreground of this 1958 photograph. Today the line is single, finishing at buffer stops close to the location of the tall signal, and the platform occupies the site of the left-hand track. When this photograph was taken, the line continued, over the level crossing and through Balloch Central Station, for another half-mile to Balloch Pier Station for interchange with the loch steamers. In 1986 the final half-mile was closed, together with both stations, and the new station was built. By that date trains had continued beyond Balloch Central only when there was a connection to be made at the pier, which meant two or three times a day in summer, but not at all in winter. Nearly all trains made Balloch Central their terminus, but the signalman still had to open or close the level crossing gates about eight times an hour, that is twice every time a train arrived or departed. So there were clear advantages in relocating the station, but this could have been done without closing the line to the pier, and in that case, with only a few trains using the crossing, and at low speeds, an ungated crossing with flashing lights would have been appropriate. That is almost exactly what was done at Ardrossan, where trains now usually run only as far as the town station, and continue to the harbour, over ungated crossings, only when there is a connection to be made with the Arran ferry.

Balloch Pier Station, looking south. This is how the station looked to passengers arriving off a steamer, although a train would be at the platform waiting for them. The photograph probably dates from the 1930s.

Jamestown Church.

Jamestown Parish Church dates from 1869 and is happily still in use. But there are now double yellow lines along the edges of the main road, and horses and carts seldom, if ever, feature among the busy traffic.

Cyclists, a pony and its rider, and pedestrians were the only traffic present on the main road through Gartocharn when this view looking west was taken around 1905. The village post office, on the right, was moved a couple of houses along the street about 1930; previously it had been run by Annie and Gracie Cooper, and this house is still owned by the Cooper family.

The Holly Bush Tea Room and antique shop was east of Gartocharn on the road to Drymen. In the 1920s it was run by a Mrs Robertson. Her son James was a talented engineer who designed a four-cylinder, two-stroke car engine. Unable to get it taken up for production during the Depression, he designed a car, which he called the 'Cowal', in which the prototype engine was installed to demonstrate its possibilities. Regrettably, this venture was equally unsuccessful. James Robertson's moment eventually came during the Second World War when he worked with Barnes Wallis's team developing the 'bouncing bomb' for the Dambusters. Although his car was eventually scrapped, his engine survives to this day in the Museum of Transport, Glasgow. Mrs Robertson's tea room and antiques business seems to have been little more successful than her son's ventures: the building is recalled around Gartocharn as having been a private house in the 1930s.

In this 1934 photograph of Balloch, the village is dominated by the then-new silk-dyeing factory. Established by a Swiss company, in 1960 it became the property of the New British Silk Dyeing Company and is still remembered as the 'B.S.D. factory'. Remembered, because this late-flowering offshoot of the Vale of Leven's traditional bleaching and dyeing industry closed in 1980. In fact, it processed many different kinds of fabrics. The location is now occupied by the approaches to Loch Lomond Shores national park gateway centre.

Today, the location of Tullichewan Castle is occupied by the dual-carriageway A82 trunk road, and resounds to the constant roar of traffic. There was a house of some sort here by the early eighteenth century, and the castle seen here was built about 1808 for John and William Stirling, textile manufacturers. The grounds were laid out by Alexander Nasmyth, best known as an artist for his portrait of Robert Burns. The house and estate passed through the hands of several wealthy industrialists, but throughout the Victorian and Edwardian periods they belonged to successive members of the Campbell family, Glasgow wholesalers of drapery, mercery and haberdashery. The castle continued to be a private residence until the Second World War when it was requisitioned to house Wrens and other naval personnel and was named H.M.S. *Tullichewan*. It was subsequently used as temporary hostel accommodation, but in the austerity of post-war Britain there was little demand for run-down ornamental castles, much more for building materials. The castle's wood panelling and roof were removed and later the building was reduced to rubble in 1954. What was then known as the Alexandria by-pass was eventually routed over its site. A stable block in similar style still overlooks the road.

Auchendennan was one of several ornate mansions built by Glasgow's merchant princes around the southern shores of Loch Lomond. It has had a happier fate than Tullichewan. Although taken over by the military during the Second World War, it was bought by the Scottish Youth Hostels Association in 1945. It was opened as the Loch Lomond Youth Hostel on 30 June of that year, and continues to fulfil that role. This photograph appeared on a postcard sent during the 1940s. The correspondent thought it was a 'super hostel', but complained that 'they give us porridge with salt in it'!

The green-and-cream electric tramcars of Dumbarton Burgh and County Tramways Co. Ltd started running to and from Balloch in 1908; their terminus adjoined Balloch Central Station. The route from Balloch was through Alexandria and Dumbarton to Dalmuir, where passengers travelling further could change into Glasgow cars or, of course, vice versa. Cars ran at twenty-minute intervals, and more frequently on Saturdays and Sundays. When introduced they were extremely popular and brought huge crowds to Balloch – the 19,000 people who arrived on the first Saturday of operation were exceeded by the 30,000 who came on the first Sunday.

By 1928, when this photograph was taken, the surroundings of Balloch tramway terminus were becoming built-up, although road traffic was evidently still sparse. However, it was around this time that the competition from motor bus operators became intense – not only were buses more flexible about their routes, but the operators had no tracks or electric overhead equipment to maintain. The tram route closed that year and the company went into liquidation.

The crowds seen here on the east bank of the River Leven, just above Balloch Bridge, may well have arrived by tram. Certainly everyone is in their Sunday best for a day out, even though boots and socks have been removed to go paddling.

A lochside picnic: the date is 16 August 1928 although the picnickers are unknown. The location is the south end of Loch Lomond; the jetty in the background adjoined the steamer slipway at Balloch Pier.

In the 1920s the River Leven at Balloch became a veritable floating village of houseboats. Such vessels are attractive when new but deteriorate rapidly; it is clear that here, as elsewhere, their condition ranged from excellent to near-derelict.

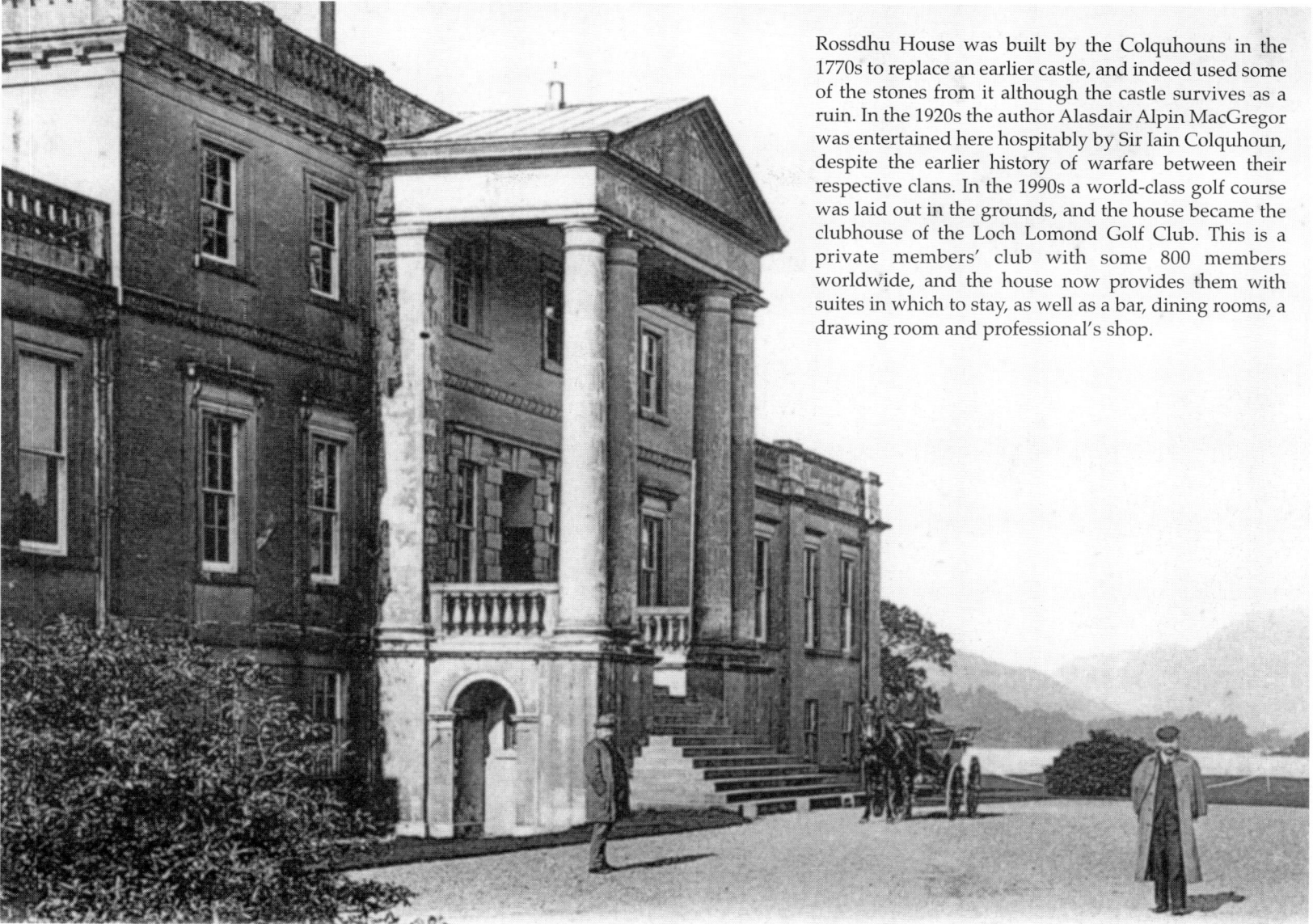

Rossdhu House was built by the Colquhouns in the 1770s to replace an earlier castle, and indeed used some of the stones from it although the castle survives as a ruin. In the 1920s the author Alasdair Alpin MacGregor was entertained here hospitably by Sir Iain Colquhoun, despite the earlier history of warfare between their respective clans. In the 1990s a world-class golf course was laid out in the grounds, and the house became the clubhouse of the Loch Lomond Golf Club. This is a private members' club with some 800 members worldwide, and the house now provides them with suites in which to stay, as well as a bar, dining rooms, a drawing room and professional's shop.

Early motorists calling at the Inverbeg Hotel. The car is a De Dion, made in France in 1903 or 1904, and registered in Dunbartonshire. From the loch shore nearby there is a ferry to Rowardennan – both this and the Hotel are old-established and both remain in business today.

The Scottish Youth Hostels Association originated in the early 1930s and one of its first hostels was at Inverbeg, opening on 22 August 1931. A new timber building was built on a site provided by Sir Iain Colquhoun of Luss. Hostellers used to cross the loch by ferry to climb Ben Lomond. By the 1990s the road up the west side of Loch Lomond had become very busy with traffic and was no longer pleasant for walking or cycling: demand for hostel accommodation at Inverbeg dropped and the hostel closed in 1994. The correspondent on this postcard, sent in the hostel's heyday, described it as being 'like a little wooden shanty in the wild and woolly west'.

Rowardennan Hotel on the east shore of the loch is still connected by ferry with Inverbeg on the west shore. Ben Lomond is in the background and the shortest route to the summit starts from here. There was a comfortable inn here by the 1830s, from which guides could be hired. By the time this photograph was taken it had been much extended and ponies could be hired too.

When a busy steamer arrived at Stronachlachar or Inversnaid, three, four or even five coaches were needed to carry tourists onward. Here, three coaches have set out in convoy from Stronachlachar – Loch Katrine is in the background – *en route* for Inversnaid.

A four-in-hand passes St Kentigerna's Church, Inversnaid – at no great speed, for a cautious approach is needed to the steep hill down to the loch. The coaches were still running in the 1930s by which time they had become a tourist attraction in themselves, but nevertheless they were withdrawn at the end of the summer season of 1937 to be replaced by buses the following summer. This coach service is believed to have been the last horsedrawn coach service to operate in Scotland.

On the east shore of the loch, a mile or so north of Inversnaid, is 'Rob Roy's Cave', which is in fact a rather uninteresting jumble of rocks and boulders among which a man might conceal himself. It acted nevertheless as a magnet to nineteenth-century tourists, perhaps not least because of the difficulties of reaching it. Usually this meant hiring a boat and boatman from Inversnaid or Tarbet; the paddle steamers also, in their early days, would lie at anchor while their passengers took a boat to go ashore. The association with Rob Roy may or may not be fictitious; there is an earlier and equally dubious association with Robert Bruce who may or may not have rested in the cave when he passed this way with his followers in 1306.

From 1817 until 1989 successive paddle steamers, and latterly a motor vessel, linked Balloch with piers up Loch Lomond. For much of this period they were used by locals and visitors alike, a convenient means of transport not only over the length of the loch but also between its east and west shores, for the steamers pursued a zig-zag course from pier to pier. In this 1920s picture the paddle steamer *Prince George* has reached Ardlui, the northern terminus of her route, and is preparing to set off south again.

Railways reached northern Loch Lomondside in 1894 with the opening of the West Highland Railway from Craigendoran, near Helensburgh, to Fort William. Here in all its brash newness is Craigenarden Viaduct, between Arrochar & Tarbet and Ardlui Stations, with the coach road and Loch Lomond below. Vegetation has long since re-clothed the hillside, and the viaduct can now only be glimpsed through the trees.

Arrochar & Tarbet Station was typical of those on the West Highland Railway. Today the line is signalled by radio links, but the signal box on the right survives as a waiting room although the signal in the distance has disappeared. The main station building has been replaced by a smaller building in the same style as the signal box.

How to dress for a ride in an open car, out of season: a fur coat was evidently well worth having. The car is a rarity, and its make has so far eluded expert identification. The location is the Tarbet Hotel, the date 1922.

Even for a closed touring car an overcoat was desirable. This car has probably been hired by visitors. It is a luxury model, almost certainly of American origin – the spare tyre with bolt-on rim, in place of a complete spare wheel, is an American feature. Cars such as this tended to be bought by the owner of the big house and then later sold on second-hand to a hotel for hiring out and taxi work. The location again is the Tarbet Hotel.